LITTLE

A Visit to
Spain

Jackie Gaff

Kingfisher Books

Contents

Welcome to Spain	5
Spain and its islands	6
In a Spanish town	8
Going shopping	10
In a café	12
Eating and drinking	14
Things to see and do	16
In the countryside	18
A visit to Madrid...	20
...and Barcelona	21
Travelling around	22
School and holidays	24
Celebrations	26
Let's speak Spanish!	28
Index	30

Welcome to Spain

A family of tourists unpacks their car in a sunny Spanish village. Brilliant red geraniums hang from the balconies of whitewashed houses. The holiday stretches ahead – long hot days for swimming from beautiful sandy beaches, trips inland to explore wild forests and pretty hilltop villages, or visits to one of Spain's many fascinating and ancient cities.

Spain and its islands

Mainland Spain is in the southwestern corner of Europe, almost surrounded by sea. Also part of Spain are the Balearic Islands and far to the south, near the coast of Africa, the Canary Islands.

A vast plain covers the centre of Spain, much of it farming land. It is broken by mountain ranges, some so high that people ski on them in winter.

SPANISH MONEY

In Spain, the money people use is called pesetas. When you go to a bank, you'll see signs that show you how much Spanish money you can get in exchange for your own money.

In a Spanish town

In the centre of most small towns and villages you'll find a *plaza* (main square), ringed with shops and cafés. Spain has long been a Catholic country and to one side of the *plaza*, there is often a church.

---

① *Cerámicas* – shop selling local pottery
② *Ultramarinos* – grocery shop
③ *Farmacia* – chemist's
④ *Panadería* – bakery   ⑤ *Banco* – bank
⑥ *Oficina de Correos* – post office

FRESH FISH

Spain is famous for its wonderful fresh seafood. At the *pescadería* (fishmonger's), look out for *boquerones* (whitebait) – these tiny fish are often fried and eaten whole. *Calamares* (squid) are also very tasty.

Life slows down in the heat of the day. Shops usually shut at lunchtime, while people eat or take a *siesta* (a nap). Places open up again in the late afternoon, finally closing at 8 pm or later.

Going shopping

Visiting a bustling street market is one of the best ways to discover what the Spanish like to eat and drink. Here, you'll find piles of fresh fruit and vegetables, and tubs of shining olives. Some stalls display different sausages, others sell nothing but *queso* (cheese). Best of all, perhaps, are the stalls selling the thin curly doughnuts called *churros*.

You'll find souvenir shops in most towns. Popular gifts are fans, pottery, dolls, guitars and *sombreros!*

monedero
purse

castañuelas
castanets

plato
plate

muñeca
doll

sombrero
hat

In a café

Cafés and bars are open all day long in Spain. People love to stop off for a coffee or a cold drink, or just to sit for a while and chat to a friend. Bar snacks called *tapas* are a real speciality – they can be anything from crisps and a few olives, to a hot or cold mini-meal.

EATING TAPAS

If you order *tapas*, you'll be able to choose from dozens of dishes, according to the part of Spain you're visiting. You may be able to try mussels, green peppers cooked in tomato, or even fried pig's ear!

Ice-cream is called *helado*. Try *helado de fresa* (strawberry), *de pistacho* or *de chocolate*.

FRUIT CUP

This cooling fruit drink is just right for hot summer days. As well as a big jug, you'll need:

1 apple, 1 orange
Strawberries
Lemonade
2 sprigs mint
Lots of ice

1 Ask a grown-up to help you chop up the apple and strawberries, and slice the orange.
2 Put everything in the jug, pouring in the lemonade last. *¡Salud!* – cheers!

Eating and drinking

In Spain, the main meal of the day is lunch. It is usually eaten late, at 2 or 3 pm. A typical lunch often has three to four courses – as well as a starter and a dessert, there may be a fish dish and a meat course.

Supper is eaten at 9 or 10 pm. This much simpler meal may be pasta or *tortilla* – a potato omelette.

On special days, breakfast might be a glass of hot chocolate and crunchy *churros*.

Many Spanish dishes are cooked in olive oil. Olives are also eaten whole as a tasty snack.

A SPANISH SANDWICH

Sandwiches are called *bocadillos*, and they're made with rolls or a chunk of crusty bread. They are filled with cheese, ham, or slices of a spicy Spanish sausage (*chorizo*), and fresh salad vegetables.

Paella is one of Spain's most famous dishes. It is made from rice, seafood and chicken, and its yellow colour comes from a spice called saffron.

Each region of Spain has its own desserts. In Galicia in the north-west, they make an unusual rice pudding, browning the top with a red-hot poker.

Things to see and do

All over Spain there are amazing castles, built hundreds of years ago for kings and nobles. With more than 1,500 castles, there's bound to be one nearby for you to visit. Some castles are now in ruins. Others have been turned into museums or grand hotels.

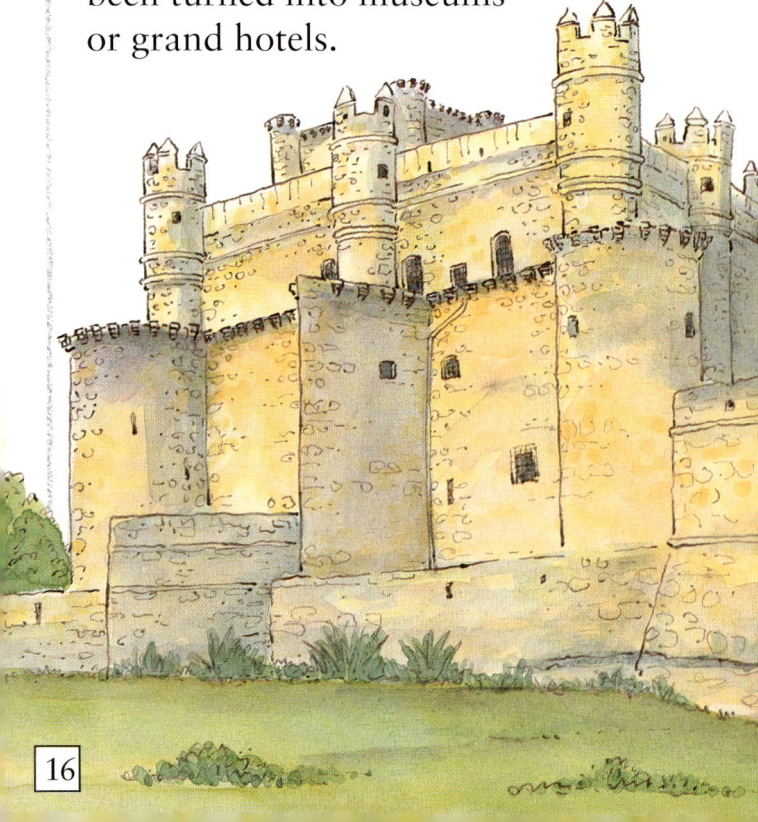

△ South of Madrid, you can see the windmills made famous by the story of Don Quixote, a knight who challenged one of them to a duel!

◁ Guadamur Castle, near Toledo.

There are things to see in Spain that are even more ancient than its castles. The stone bulls of Guisando, near Avila, were carved thousands of years ago.

17

In the countryside

Summers in southern Spain are baking hot – perfect for olive trees. Late in the year, the branches are beaten to knock down the ripe olives. Some are bottled or canned. Others are crushed and squeezed into oil. Grapes also thrive in Spain's sunny weather and lots of good wine is made here.

DONKEY WORK

In some parts of Spain, people still use donkeys to help with farm work. The donkeys may be harnessed so that they can pull heavy carts or, like the one in this picture, they may carry baskets called panniers on their backs.

Grapes are picked in early autumn, then pressed to make wine.

A visit to Madrid...

Madrid has been the capital of Spain for over 400 years. It has many fine buildings, museums and art galleries such as the Prado. There are parks to walk in, too. At the city's heart is a huge square called the Plaza Mayor.

▽ Long ago, the Plaza Mayor was where Spanish kings and queens were crowned. It was also used for bullfights.

△ Not far from the Plaza Mayor is the Royal Palace. The King and Queen don't live there, but they use it for important banquets.

...and Barcelona

The second biggest Spanish city is Barcelona, on the northeast coast. A famous tree-lined avenue called the Rambla leads from the harbour right into the city's heart. Packed with cafés and flower shops, the Rambla is a favourite place for an evening stroll, or *paseo*.

The Sagrada Familia is a fairytale cathedral, designed by Antonio Gaudí.

Travelling around

Spain is a large country and, after Switzerland, the most mountainous in Europe. Although smaller roads can be windy and slow, there is little traffic on them. Motorways, called *autopistas*, are a fast route between big cities.

Taking a local bus is one of the best ways of exploring a town. You pay as you board. Madrid and Barcelona also have underground trains.

A CABLE CAR RIDE

If you visit Barcelona, you could take the cable car that runs right across the harbour all the way up to the top of Montjuïc – a mountain with museums and a park on top. You'll get a spectacular view over the city as you ride.

The most peaceful way to travel is on horseback, well away from cars and roads. The region of Andalucía in the south is famous for its beautiful horses, and riding holidays are always very popular here.

School and holidays

School in Spain lasts from 9 am to 5 pm, with an hour-and-a-half break for lunch. Summers are far too hot for sitting in a classroom, and the holiday lasts from June to September. There's lots of time for enjoying outdoor games like *pelota*.

Pelota is said to be the world's fastest ball game. It can be played against a wall, but there are special courts, too. In a version of the game called *cesta*, each player has a curved basket to throw and catch the ball.

The most popular sport in Spain is probably soccer. Madrid and Barcelona both have world-famous soccer teams.

PLAY CHAPAS

Here's a game that schoolchildren play in breaks. All you need are some metal bottle tops and a different coloured paper for each player.

1 Cut out circles of paper to fit in your bottle tops and glue them inside.

2 Take turns flicking the tops against a wall. The player whose tops land closest to the wall wins, scooping up everyone else's.

Celebrations

Festivals are called *fiestas* in Spain and most cities, towns and villages have their own special ones. Often, a *fiesta* celebrates the birthday of a special saint or a famous person, with fireworks and fun-fairs. Sometimes, people dress up in huge papier-mâché costumes. The celebrations usually carry on long into the night.

MAKE CASTANETS

You'll need some wallpaper paste, card, newspapers, black poster paint, clear varnish, and a ribbon.

1 Mix a bowl of paste and cut two castanet shapes out of card.
2 Tear eight pages of paper into small strips. Dip them in paste and smooth them over the cards. Add several layers, leaving each one to dry, until you have the rounded shape shown below.
3 Make a hole in the top of each castanet.
4 Paint and varnish the castanets, then thread ribbon through the holes to tie them together.

In the south, you may see women and men dancing the *flamenco*, stamping their feet and clicking castanets to guitar music.

Let's speak Spanish!

NUMBERS	
1	Uno
2	Dos
3	Tres
4	Cuatro
5	Cinco
6	Seis
7	Siete
8	Ocho
9	Nueve
10	Diez

Buenos días
Hello

Por favor
Please

Gracias
Thank you

Quiero un helado, por favor.
I'd like an ice-cream, please.
¿Cuánto cuesta éste?
How much is this one?

¿Habla inglés?
Do you speak English?

No
No

Sí
Yes

Index

Balearic islands 6, 7
Barcelona 7, 21, 23

cable car 23
café 12
Canary Islands 6
castanets 27
castle 16-17,

donkey 19
drinks 12, 13

fiesta 26
flamenco dancing 27
food 9, 10, 12-15

Gaudí Antonio 21
geography 6-7
grapes 18, 19

horse-riding 23

ice-cream 13

Madrid 7, 20, 25
map 7
market 10
money 6

olives 14, 18

paella 15
pelota 24-25
plaza 8
Plaza Mayor 20
Prado museum 20

school 24
shopping 8-9, 10-11
siesta 9
sightseeing 16-21
sport 25

tapas 12
transport 22-23

windmill 17